Usborne

London

Quiz Book

Simon Tudhope

Illustrated by Clair Rossiter

Designed by Kate Rimmer

1 Which is a traditional London food?

    a) jellied eels

    b) stewed starfish

    c) pickled jellyfish

2 London is the biggest city in Europe.
True or false?

3 What's the nickname for
the big clock tower at the
Houses of Parliament?

    a) Big Ken

    b) Big Ben

    c) Big Bob

4 What's the police headquarters in London called?

    a) England Yard   b) Scotland Yard   c) Wales Yard

5 Which accent comes from the East End of London?

    a) Geordie   b) Brummie   c) Cockney

6 My friend is Dr. Watson,
and my enemy is the Napoleon of crime.
I live at 221b Baker Street, London.

Who am I?

7 Which Premier League team plays at the Emirates Stadium?

a) Tottenham Hotspur

b) Chelsea

c) Arsenal

8 Complete the line chanted on Bonfire Night about
the attempt to blow up the Houses of Parliament
in 1605:

"Remember, remember the 5th of November...

a) thirty-three traitors were shot."

b) dungeons and witches and rot."

c) gunpowder, treason and plot."

9 On average, what's London's hottest month?

a) May   b) July   c) September

10 Which river flows through the middle of London?

a) Thames   b) Severn   c) Seine

11 Which mysterious criminal terrorized
the streets of London in the 1880s?

a) Jack the Ripper

b) the Artful Dodger

c) Professor Moriarty

1 **Which TV broadcaster has its headquarters in London?**

    a) ABC   b) BBC   c) CNN

2 **When the Romans invaded Britain in 43 AD, what did they call the settlement that's now called London?**

    a) Nova Roma   b) Londinium   c) Rainalotta

3 **Where are the Crown Jewels kept?**

    a) Tower of London
    b) Bank of England
    c) Windsor Castle

4 **Which of these statements about the London Underground is true?**

    a) it's the world's oldest underground system
    b) it's the world's busiest underground system
    c) it's the world's longest underground system

5 **What's the name of the ceremony that takes place when new guards come on duty outside Buckingham Palace?**

    a) Turning the Troop
    b) Switching the Watch
    c) Changing the Guard

6 **Who was created by London writer Ian Fleming?**

    a) Peter Pan   b) Oliver Twist   c) James Bond

7 How long does a ride last on this
giant Ferris wheel in the middle of London?

    a) 10 minutes   b) 30 minutes   c) 1 hour

8 Buckingham Palace was never hit by a bomb during
the Second World War.

    True or false?

9 Where can you 'meet' Jack Sheppard, the thief who
became a popular hero after escaping from prison
four times in 1724?

    a) Tower of London
    b) The London Dungeon
    c) Imperial War Museum

10 What's the name of the travelcard you can use on
London public transport?

    a) Oyster Card   b) Lobster Card   c) Cockle Card

(1) I eat snozzcumbers and drink frobscottle, which gives you giant whizzpoppers! I had breakfast at Buckingham Palace.
Who am I?

(2) Which sport was most popular in Roman London?
   a) football   b) gladiator fighting   c) darts

(3) In 1013 a Viking army captured London, led by their king, Sweyn...
   a) Forkbeard   b) Knifebeard   c) Spoonbeard

(4) The City of London is the smallest city in England.
True or false?

(5) There are two flags that can be flown above Buckingham Palace. Match each one to the correct occasion.
   a) Union Flag
   b) Royal Standard

1) The Queen is staying at Buckingham Palace
2) The Queen is away from Buckingham Palace

6 Which country donates the Christmas tree that's put up in Trafalgar Square every year?

a) India   b) Russia   c) Norway

7 What are the hats called that the guards of Buckingham Palace wear?

a) Wolfskins
b) Bearskins
c) Sheepskins

8 Which is NOT a character created by London-born writer Beatrix Potter?

a) Jemima Puddle-Duck
b) Mrs. Tiggy-Winkle
c) Farmer Bumpkin

9 When *Monopoly* first came out in 1935, the most expensive property was Mayfair, at £400. Roughly how much would a property in Mayfair cost today?

a) £2,500   b) £250,000   c) £2,500,000

10 Which street in east London is famous for its curry houses, its bustling market and its street art?

a) Brick Lane   b) Stone Lane   c) Pebble Lane

1 **What's the name of the busy motorway that circles London?**

   a) A5   b) M25   c) B515

2 **The writer Mary Shelley was born in London in 1797. Which tormented monster did she create?**

   a) Mr. Hyde   b) Voldemort   c) Frankenstein's monster

3 **Complete the name of the big show that's held in an area of London called Chelsea every year: Chelsea .... Show.**

   a) Flower   b) Dog   c) Yacht

4 **What's kept inside the Tate Modern building?**

   a) designer clothes
   b) modern art
   c) antiques

(5) Which phrase is used to say that the roads are very busy?
   a) "It's like Portobello Market."
   b) "It's like Piccadilly Circus."
   c) "It's like Waterloo Station."

(6) Where does the Prime Minister live?
   a) 10 Fleet Street
   b) 10 Bond Street
   c) 10 Downing Street

(7) ... And which of these Prime Ministers lived there the longest?
   a) Tony Blair
   b) Winston Churchill
   c) Margaret Thatcher

(8) In an average year in London, which month gets the least amount of rain?
   a) February   b) June   c) August

(9) Which of these sports does the Queen like best?
   a) horse racing
   b) boxing
   c) rugby

1. In which London department store can you buy a solid crystal bathtub, a gold golf putter and a diamond-encrusted tea bag?
   a) Harrods
   b) Fortnum & Mason
   c) Wilko

2. Where does the Queen spend the most nights each year?
   a) St James's Palace
   b) Windsor Castle
   c) Buckingham Palace

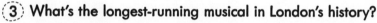

3. What's the longest-running musical in London's history?
   a) *Grease*   b) *Les Misérables*   c) *Wicked*

4. What's the most popular tourist attraction in London?
   a) Natural History Museum
   b) St Paul's Cathedral
   c) British Museum

5. Which London-born actor plays Rey in the *Star Wars* movies?
   a) Cara Delevingne
   b) Carey Mulligan
   c) Daisy Ridley

6. Big Ben's bell weighs the same as:
   a) an elephant
   b) a double-decker bus
   c) a jumbo jet

7 What percentage of the London Underground system is underground?

a) 45% b) 75% c) 99%

8 In 1894, *The Times* newspaper predicted that in 50 years' time, London would be buried under 9ft (2.75m) of what?

a) water b) coal dust c) horse manure

9 Which fruit completes the title of the nursery rhyme about church bells in London? .... *and Lemons.*

a) Oranges b) Apples c) Bananas

10 Which type of animal can you NOT see at the London aquarium?

a) sharks
b) whales
c) penguins

1 Which fictional character works for MI6, but is rarely seen at the headquarters in London?

a) Jason Bourne   b) Doctor Who   c) James Bond

2 What's the name of this cathedral in the heart of London?

a) St Peter's   b) St Paul's   c) St John's

3 ... And who designed it in the 1600s?

a) Christopher Robin
b) Christopher Sparrow
c) Christopher Wren

4 If you meet the Queen, you should address her as Your...

a) Majesty   b) Highness   c) Grace

5 In which fictional London borough is the TV soap
EastEnders set?

a) Walton   b) Wallaby   c) Walford

6 People move to London from all over the world. Roughly
how many different languages are spoken there?

a) 50   b) 300   c) 1,000

7 I used to fly to a house in London
to listen to bedtime stories.
One night I was spotted and flew off so quickly
I left my shadow behind.

Who am I?

8 Which is the odd one out?

Waterloo, Paddington, Knightsbridge, Marylebone

9 Which former England soccer player never
played for a London club?

a) Steven Gerrard
b) Rio Ferdinand
c) John Terry

10 Large flocks of which bird
peck at the crumbs dropped
by London sightseers?

a) pigeons
b) robins
c) ravens

1 Which event was this spiky building built to celebrate?

    a) the millennium

    b) the Queen's coronation

    c) the moon landing

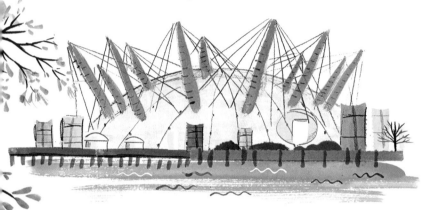

2 More people live in London than any other city in Europe.
True or false?

3 What feature makes Wembley Stadium visible from
miles around?

    a) a giant statue   b) two tall towers   c) a huge arch

4 I fly when I open my umbrella,
and my friend is a cheerful cockney chimney sweep.
I think a spoonful of sugar helps the medicine go down.
Who am I?

5 Where was the capital of England
before London?

    a) Edinburgh

    b) Colchester

    c) Liverpool

6 People travel to London from all over the world. Match each city with its distance from London.

a) Los Angeles   1) 2,184 miles (3,515km)

b) Madrid   2) 786 miles (1,265km)

c) Cairo   3) 5,447 miles (8,765km)

7 Which team plays its home matches at a stadium built for the 2012 Olympic Games?

a) Leicester City

b) West Ham United

c) Manchester United

8 What are you NOT likely to see on the River Thames?

a) tug boats

b) ferries

c) gondolas

9 Where can you see the world's largest collection of plants, with over 30,000 species?

a) Bushy Park   b) Regent's Park   c) Kew Gardens

10 All the properties on a standard British *Monopoly* board are places in London.

True or false?

11 What was the nickname for the flying bombs that struck London during the Second World War?

a) doodlebugs   b) jitterbugs   c) fireflies

1 **What's the nickname for this part of London?**
   a) Chinatown   b) Japantown   c) Little Italy

2 **Who holds a competition every year where anyone in the world can submit an artwork and the best 1,000 go on display?**
   a) Royal Academy   b) National Gallery   c) BBC

3 **Which London square hosts lots of film premieres?**
   a) Trafalgar Square
   b) Russell Square
   c) Leicester Square

4 **Who were the last invaders to capture London?**
   a) Romans   b) Normans   c) Vikings

5 **... And when did they do it?**
   a) 844   b) 1066   c) 1288

6 Match the phrase for 'welcome to London' with the language it's from.

a) Bienvenue à Londres

b) 欢迎来到伦敦

c) Witamy w Londynie

1) Chinese

2) Polish

3) French

7 When did England win the FIFA World Cup at Wembley Stadium?

a) 1933   b) 1966   c) 1999

8 The Queen owns Buckingham Palace.

True or false?

9 Which fictional bear was found at a London train station, and has a particular liking for English marmalade?

a) Paddington   b) Yogi   c) Baloo

10 What's the name of the plague that killed half the people in London between 1348 and 1350?

a) Red Death   b) White Death   c) Black Death

1 Which bridge in London has two tall towers and splits in the middle to allow ships to pass through?

a) the Millennium Bridge

b) London Bridge

c) Tower Bridge

2 Which sport is played at the Wimbledon championships?

a) football   b) tennis   c) rugby

3 ... And when did the first championship take place?

a) 1777   b) 1877   c) 1977

4 There are two 'houses' in the Houses of Parliament. One is the House of Commons. What's the other?

a) The House of Uncommons

b) The House of Lords

c) The House of Cards

5. In the opening ceremony of the 2012 Olympic Games, which bumbling character joined the London Symphony Orchestra and played one note on his keyboard throughout the whole performance?

a) Mr. Bean   b) Mr. Bacon   c) Mr. Butter

6. Which bird would you never see on London rooftops?

a) pigeon   b) gull   c) emu

7. Every year since 1856, a boat race has taken place on the River Thames between which two university teams?

a) Oxford and Cambridge
b) Glasgow and Edinburgh
c) Manchester and Liverpool

8. What destroyed central London in 1666?

a) fire   b) earthquake   c) flood

9. I was born in London, but have also lived in Los Angeles. I was in a world-famous girl band where my nickname was Posh Spice.

Who am I?

1 Where's the FA Cup final played?

a) Wembley Stadium
b) Stamford Bridge
c) Craven Cottage

2 Who was the 'British Bulldog' who worked in 10 Downing Street during the Second World War?

a) David Lloyd George
b) Winston Churchill
c) King George VI

3 The world-famous classical music concerts held in London each summer are called The...

a) Galas   b) Proms   c) Crufts

4 There's a dome in London that's so wide it could cover four buses lined up end to end. But if you're standing inside, you can hear the faintest whisper all around its curved walls. Where is the dome?

a) Natural History Museum
b) Westminster Abbey
c) St Paul's Cathedral

5 Which ocean does the River Thames flow into?

    a) Atlantic   b) Pacific   c) Arctic

6 What caused the Great Stink of 1858?

    a) sewage in the River Thames

    b) horse manure on the streets

    c) piles of rotting food

7 After British, what's the most common nationality of people living in London?

    a) Polish   b) Indian   c) Italian

8 ... And what percentage of Londoners are from that country?

    a) 3.4 %   b) 13.4%   c) 23.4%

9 What's the name of the place where you'll find lots of street entertainers?

    a) Covent Yard

    b) Covent Park

    c) Covent Garden

10 From 1305 to 1772, what were displayed on London Bridge?

    a) exotic animals

    b) the crown jewels

    c) the heads of traitors

1 There's a statue of Horatio Nelson in central London. Who was he?

a) a knight

b) a sailor

c) a pilot

2 ... And which battle is Nelson famous for winning?

a) Battle of Trafalgar

b) Battle of Waterloo

c) Battle of Britain

3 Which is NOT a building where the Royal Family lives?

a) Buckingham Palace

b) Crystal Palace

c) Windsor Castle

4 Which is a park in London?

a) Central Park

b) Yellowstone Park

c) Richmond Park

5 What's the main industry in the City of London?

a) car making   b) mining   c) banking

6 Match the London club to the area of the city it's from.

a) Chelsea   1) north

b) Crystal Palace   2) south

c) Tottenham Hotspur   3) east

d) West Ham United   4) west

7 Where can you see treasures from Ancient Egypt?
   a) The Natural History Museum
   b) The Imperial War Museum
   c) The British Museum

8 I'm an orphan who ran away to London.
On my way there I met the Artful Dodger,
who tricked me into joining a gang of pickpockets.
Who am I?

9 What's the name of the
London hotel that's famous
for its afternoon tea?
   a) The Ritz
   b) The Glitz
   c) The Britz

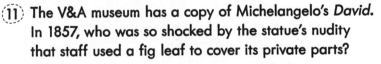

10 Which criminals were
hanged at Execution Dock,
by the River Thames?
   a) spies
   b) pirates
   c) highwaymen

11 The V&A museum has a copy of Michelangelo's *David*.
In 1857, who was so shocked by the statue's nudity
that staff used a fig leaf to cover its private parts?
   a) the Queen   b) the Pope   c) the Prime Minister

12 What side of the road do people drive on in London:
left or right?

1 **Which is NOT the nickname of a London skyscraper?**

a) broomstick   b) cheese grater   c) walkie-talkie

2 **Who was the 'Iron Lady' who lived in 10 Downing Street during the 1980s?**

a) Princess Diana

b) an old tabby cat

c) Margaret Thatcher

3 **London is the biggest city in the UK.**

True or false?

4 **The writer Ian Fleming gave James Bond the codename 007 because it was...**

a) the end of Fleming's phone number

b) the number of the bus Fleming caught to London

c) Fleming's own codename when he was in the navy

5 **The Prime Minister has keys to 10 Downing Street.**

True or false?

6 At Bankside there's a full-size replica of the ship that Sir Francis Drake sailed around the world over 400 years ago. What's the ship called?

a) *Golden Hind*   b) *Mayflower*   c) *Titanic*

7 Which queen supposedly said to a cheeky officer: "We are not amused"?

a) Anne
b) Victoria
c) Elizabeth I

8 Which animal are you unlikely to see on London streets?

a) fox
b) squirrel
c) raccoon

9 What's traditionally made on Savile Row?

a) watches   b) suits   c) gravestones

10 How many people were killed by the Great Smog that smothered London in 1952?

a) 120   b) 1,200   c) 12,000

11 Who invades London in *The War of the Worlds*, written by H.G. Wells?

a) Martians
b) dinosaurs
c) super-intelligent apes

1 Is the sign for the London Underground:
a red circle with a blue bar **or**
a blue circle with a red bar?

2 Since 1066, every coronation of an English monarch has taken place at this building. What's it called?
a) Northminster Abbey
b) Eastminster Abbey
c) Westminster Abbey

3 It's illegal to stick a postage stamp with the Queen's head on it upside down.
True or false?

4 Which people were living by the River Thames before the Romans built Londinium?
a) Celts   b) Saxons   c) Vikings

5 What do you put inside the big red boxes that stand on London pavements?
a) letters   b) old clothes   c) litter

6 How many bedrooms does Buckingham Palace have?

    a) 40   b) 120   c) 240

7 What giant structure was built to protect London from disaster?

    a) Highgate Wind Barrier

    b) Thames Flood Barrier

    c) Putney Fire Barrier

8 What's the name of the Londoners who wear these sparkly hats?

    a) Pearly King and Queen

    b) Morris Dancers

    c) Big Chiefs

9 During a spell of madness, which English king stood up in the Houses of Parliament and began his speech: "My Lords and peacocks"?

    a) Richard II   b) George III   c) Edward VIII

10 Who rides in a golden carriage once a year through the streets of London?

    a) the Prime Minister

    b) the Lord Mayor

    c) the Queen

11 London was the first city in the world to have over five million people.

True or false?

1 An elephant was brought to London Zoo in 1865 and its name quickly became slang for anything very large. What was it called?

    a) Jumbo   b) Mammoth   c) Titanic

2 Which is NOT a real station on the London Underground?

    a) Elephant and Castle
    b) Shepherd's Bush
    c) Pilgrim's Cross

3 On Christmas Day 1066, who was crowned King of England at Westminster Abbey?

    a) Henry VIII
    b) Charles I
    c) William the Conqueror

4 What was the dominant language in London during Roman times?

    a) Greek   b) Latin   c) Egyptian

5 Where's the most expensive place to open a shop in London?

    a) King's Road   b) Bond Street   c) Carnaby Street

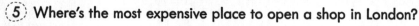

6 On average, London is colder than Paris in winter.
True or false?

7 ...And hotter than Paris in summer.
True or false?

8 Which of these teams is NOT
based in London?
a) Charlton Athletic
b) Queens Park Rangers
c) Wolverhampton Wanderers

9 Which scientist visited the first ever orangutan
at London Zoo, and was amazed by the
human-like way it behaved?
a) Charles Darwin
b) Albert Einstein
c) Marie Curie

10 Which breed of dog
does the Queen keep?
a) Welsh Corgi
b) British Bulldog
c) Yorkshire Terrier

11 Who tried to blow up the Houses of Parliament in 1605?
a) Oliver Cromwell
b) Guy Fawkes
c) Robin Hood

1 Many of the grand buildings in London are designed to look like buildings from which ancient civilization?

a) Ancient Greece
b) Ancient Egypt
c) Ancient Persia

2 What did Elizabeth II train as before she became Queen?

a) hairdresser   b) mechanic   c) nurse

3 I am a bear of very little brain, and my best friends are Christopher Robin and Piglet. My adventures were written down by A.A. Milne, who was born in London.

Who am I?

4 The Great Fire of London burned much of the city to the ground. Where did the fire start?

a) a pub   b) a prison   c) a bakery

5 ... And how many people did it officially kill?

a) 6   b) 600   c) 60,000

6 Match these famous Londoners to their profession:

a) David Attenborough   1) singer

b) David Beckham   2) inventor

c) Tim Berners-Lee   3) wildlife expert

d) Adele   4) soccer player

7 Where can you visit Dinosaur Island, which has the world's first life-size models of dinosaurs?

a) Crystal Palace Park

b) Windsor Great Park

c) Hampstead Heath

8 Where can you see the painting *Sunflowers,* by Vincent van Gogh?

a) National Portrait Gallery

b) National Gallery

c) Tate Modern

9 Which of these movies is NOT set in London?

a) *Mary Poppins*

b) *101 Dalmatians*

c) *The Wizard of Oz*

10 Where would you go to watch musicals like *Les Misérables* or *Grease*?

a) Camden Town

b) West End

c) Brixton

1. **From Euston Station in the middle of London, which taxi ride would cost the most?**
   a) to Heathrow Airport
   b) to the British Museum
   c) to Trafalgar Square

2. **London is the wettest capital city in Europe.**
   True or false?

3. **What spectacular stunt did the Queen appear to perform in the opening ceremony for the London 2012 Olympics?**
   a) skydive into the stadium
   b) waterski along the River Thames
   c) ride a motorcycle through a ring of fire

4. **According to the story, what unlikely objects gave a young servant called Dick Whittington the message that one day he would be Mayor of London?**
   a) the stars   b) church bells   c) a flock of starlings

5. **What's "falling down" in the popular nursery rhyme?**
   a) Windsor Castle
   b) London Bridge
   c) House of Lords

6. **I was born in Fulham in London in 1989, and am famous for playing a wizard who wears glasses even though I don't need glasses myself.**
   Who am I?

7 **Which England striker was born in London?**

a) Wayne Rooney b) Alan Shearer c) Harry Kane

8 **It's illegal to...**

a) cross Tower Bridge riding a horse
b) wear shoes without socks in Buckingham Palace
c) wear a knight's metal suit in the Houses of Parliament

9 **What's traditionally eaten at the Wimbledon championships?**

a) strawberries and cream
b) crackers and cheese
c) fish and chips

10 **To help fund Great Ormond Street children's hospital, the writer J.M. Barrie gave it the copyright to which fictional character?**

a) Paddington Bear b) Peter Pan c) Spiderman

11 **In London, what number should you call for the police, an ambulance or the fire department?**

a) 111
b) 333
c) 999

1 Which statement about the British Library is false?

    a) it has the largest collection of books in the world

    b) it has a copy of every book published in the UK

    c) it has nearly 400 miles (650km) of shelves

2 The ancient Celtic name for the River Thames was 'Tamesas'. Which is the closest translation?

    a) shallow waters   b) still waters   c) dark waters

3 The V&A is the short name for the Victoria & Albert Museum. Who were Victoria and Albert?

    a) the Queen and her husband

    b) the museum's pet cats

    c) the patron saints of London

4 Before being beheaded at the Tower of London in 1536, who laughed and said "I heard say the executioner is very good, and I have a little neck"?

    a) Guy Fawkes   b) Anne Boleyn   c) Oliver Cromwell

5 During the early 1800s, how young were some of the children working in London's factories?

    a) 4   b) 8   c) 12

6 How many people use the London Underground each year?

    a) 13 million   b) 130 million   c) 1.3 billion

7 The heavy bombing of London during the Second World War was called The...

a) Panzer
b) Colditz
c) Blitz

8 ... And how many people did it kill?

a) two thousand
b) twenty thousand
c) two hundred thousand

9 Which is the Queen's official London home, which hosts many royal events?

a) Buckingham Palace
b) Kensington Palace
c) Windsor Castle

10 Where's the big rescue shelter for dogs and cats in south London?

a) Barking   b) Battersea   c) Isle of Dogs

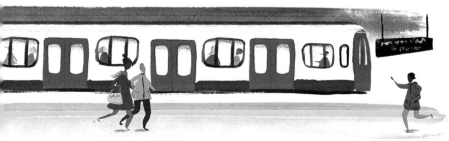

1 What's the name of the lake in Hyde Park that hosts a swimming race on Christmas Day?

a) The Lizardine   b) The Serpentine   c) The Dinotine

2 The Queen of the United Kingdom is also the Queen of 15 other countries. Which is NOT one of them?

a) Australia   b) Canada   c) United States

3 What are politicians allowed to do when debating in the House of Commons?

a) shout   b) clap   c) call someone a liar

4 Which department store in London is famous for its stylish fabric designs?

a) Liberty
b) Debenhams
c) John Lewis

5 From which London station can you catch a train to Paris?

    a) Euston

    b) Paddington

    c) St Pancras

6 ... And how long does it take?

    a) 1 hour 15 minutes

    b) 2 hours 15 minutes

    c) 5 hours 15 minutes

7 What links the Tower of London, Newgate and the Marshalsea?

    a) they're all castles

    b) they're all former prisons

    c) they're all major tourist attractions

8 What's a London slang word for a girlfriend?

    a) treacle   b) toffee   c) pudding

9 In the opening ceremony of the 2012 Olympic Games, the figure of Voldemort appeared, and he was as tall as a tree. 32 versions of which character flew down to defeat him?

    a) Harry Potter   b) Peter Pan   c) Mary Poppins

10 These big birds live in St James's Park. What are they called?

    a) penguins

    b) pelicans

    c) toucans

1 **Which is a real street in London?**

a) Ha-Ha Road   b) Ho-Ho Road   c) He-He Road

2 **The City of London is a tiny city in the heart of Greater London. Which of these statements about it is false?**

a) it has its own police force

b) it has its own mayor

c) it has its own monarch

3 **Who had the Tower of London built in 1078?**

a) Richard the Lionheart

b) William the Conqueror

c) Alfred the Great

4 **What's the nickname for the tower at 30 St Mary Axe?**

a) the sausage

b) the gherkin

c) the cigar

5 **London's double-decker buses are...**

a) red

b) green

c) blue

6 **The Queen has two birthdays.**

True or false?

7 What caused the thick, yellow fog that used to smother London's streets?

a) heavy rain   b) coal fires   c) steaming horse dung

8 ... And what was the nickname for the fog?

a) chicken-souper
b) mushroom-souper
c) pea-souper

9 Which London-born actor is famous for his roles as Sherlock Holmes and Doctor Strange?

a) Idris Elba
b) Tom Hardy
c) Benedict Cumberbatch

10 Who is NOT buried in Poets' Corner in Westminster Abbey?

a) William Shakespeare
b) Charles Dickens
c) Rudyard Kipling

11 What's the name of the stadium in London that's known as the 'home of cricket'?

a) Duke's   b) Lord's   c) Earl's

12 What giant animal skeleton looms over the entrance hall at the Natural History Museum?

a) elephant   b) *Diplodocus*   c) blue whale

1 Which item is lost most frequently on the London Underground?

  a) wallet   b) umbrella   c) mobile phone

2 Which store ejected an entire soccer team for wearing tracksuits?

  a) Marks & Spencer   b) Harrods   c) Primark

3 From which station did the *Hogwarts Express* depart?

  a) King's Cross   b) Marylebone   c) Waterloo

4 What's the London Eye?

  a) a secret surveillance network
  b) a London newspaper
  c) a giant Ferris wheel

5 I was born into poverty in south London,
but became a silent film actor
who played a tramp with a bowler hat and a funny walk.
Who am I?

6 Six ravens are always kept at the Tower of London. According to legend, what will happen if they leave?

  a) there'll be seven years of bad luck
  b) a dragon will awaken beneath the Tower
  c) the Kingdom of Great Britain will fall

7 Which headless figure is said to haunt the Tower of London?

   a) Charles I

   b) Anne Boleyn

   c) Blackbeard

8 The Queen is allowed to drive without a licence.

True or false?

9 At the 2012 Olympic Games in London, who won gold in both the 100m and 200m?

   a) Usain Bolt   b) Justin Gatlin   c) Maurice Greene

10 Where can you see one of the only surviving copies of Magna Carta, one of Leonardo da Vinci's notebooks, and every *Beano* magazine ever published?

   a) The British Library

   b) The British Museum

   c) The National Gallery

1 Where does the England rugby team play its home matches?

a) Twickenham
b) Murrayfield
c) Trent Bridge

2 What do the guards of Buckingham Palace shout if anyone gets too close?

a) "Trespassers will be shot!"
b) "Stand back from the Queen's guard!"
c) nothing – they're not allowed to speak

3 On his horse Black Bess, which outlaw is said to have ridden over 200 miles (320km) from London to York in a single night?

a) Dick Turpin   b) Robin Hood   c) Captain Kidd

4 Up until the 1700s, which bridge had public toilets that emptied straight into the River Thames?

a) the Millennium Bridge
b) Tower Bridge
c) London Bridge

5 Borough Market is a big food market in central London. In 2014 it celebrated its...

a) 10th birthday
b) 100th birthday
c) 1,000th birthday

6 What's the name of the London market that's famous for its antiques?

a) Piccadilly Market
b) Portobello Market
c) Pimlico Market

7 According to the stories, what did Mrs. Lovett put in the meat pies that she sold from her bakery on Fleet Street?

a) cats　　　　b) rats　　　　c) people

8 When politicians are debating in the House of Commons, what do they say when they agree with someone?

a) hear hear　　　b) there there　　　c) ho ho

9 Who turned into the monstrous Mr. Hyde by drinking a potion he'd concocted in his London laboratory?

a) Bruce Banner
b) Doctor Jekyll
c) Doctor Frankenstein

1. The London Marathon is held every year in April. How far do the athletes run?
   a) 16.2 miles (26km)
   b) 26.2 miles (42.2km)
   c) 36.2 miles (58.3km)

2. London is in the north of England.
   True or false?

3. What type of boat is used in the Oxford and Cambridge university boat race on the River Thames?
   a) row boat   b) yacht   c) speed boat

4. How much of the world's land is ruled by the Queen?
   a) 7%   b) 17%   c) 70%

5. What's the Fortnum & Mason department store mainly known for?
   a) clothes   b) furniture   c) food

6. The Queen has an official poet, called the 'poet laureate' who writes poems for special occasions. Their salary is £5,750 and...
   a) a barrel of sherry
   b) a barrel of beer
   c) a barrel of eels

7 London was the largest city in the world from 1831 until when?

a) 1885   b) 1925   c) 1975

8 What can you NOT find inside Buckingham Palace?

a) a post office
b) a bowling alley
c) a doctor's surgery

9 Who's done lots of graffiti art in London?

Banksy or Pudsey?

10 This tower was built for the London 2012 Olympic Games, and is the world's highest:

a) swimming pool
b) rollercoaster
c) tunnel slide

11 Where can you see a statue of Peter Pan?

a) Covent Garden
b) Kew Gardens
c) Kensington Gardens

12 What did Henry III keep in the Tower of London in the 1200s?

a) a polar bear
b) a panda
c) a koala

1 After the Norman conquest in 1066, which language was spoken at the royal court in London?

a) French   b) German   c) English

2 The Shard is the tallest building in Europe.
True or false?

3 ... And how long does it take to clean all its windows?

a) three days
b) three weeks
c) three months

4 What's the name of a rugby team that plays its home games in London?

a) Saracens
b) Crusaders
c) Cossacks

5 A loaf of bread costs more in London than it does in Manchester.
True or false?

6 Most London taxis are...

a) yellow
b) black
c) silver

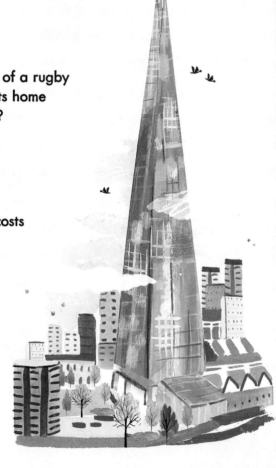

7 Which of London's airports is the busiest in Europe?

a) Heathrow
b) Gatwick
c) Stansted

8 King Charles I was executed outside the Palace of Whitehall in 1649. How was he killed?

a) hanged   b) shot   c) beheaded

9 London taxi drivers have their own slang for different place names. Match the slang to the location.

a) Gasworks   1) Natural History Museum
b) Den of Thieves   2) Houses of Parliament
c) Dead Zoo   3) London Stock Exchange

10 What's the Palace of Westminster normally called?

a) Westminster Abbey
b) The Houses of Parliament
c) The Tower of London

11 What rule must tennis players follow when choosing their outfit for Wimbledon?

a) it must be mainly white
b) it must be made from cotton
c) it must have no sponsor's logo

12 Roughly how many strawberries are eaten at the Wimbledon championships each year?

a) 12 thousand   b) 120 thousand   c) 1.2 million

1 Covent Garden is a large garden in the middle of London.
True or false?

2 Why do many historians believe that Joseph Bazalgette
saved more lives than any other person in the 1800s?
a) he discovered penicillin
b) he caught Jack the Ripper
c) he built London's sewerage system

3 I am one of the fastest sailing ships ever built,
and used to carry tea all the way from China.
Now I'm retired and on display in London.
What am I?

4 What's the average speed of the trains
on the London Underground?
a) 20mph (32km/h)
b) 40mph (64km/h)
c) 60mph (97km/h)

5 What's the name of the big
London street carnival that
takes place every year?
a) Primrose Hill Carnival
b) Notting Hill Carnival
c) Muswell Hill Carnival

6 Who tried to steal the Crown Jewels in 1671?

    a) Colonel Blood

    b) Captain Gore

    c) Commander Bones

7 ... And what did the King do when he was caught?

    a) had him executed for high treason

    b) locked him up for life in the Tower of London

    c) rewarded him with land worth £500 a year

8 Which type of music was created in east London in the early 2000s?

    a) Britpop   b) punk rock   c) grime

9 Who once said, "I don't think there will be a woman Prime Minister in my lifetime"?

    a) Winston Churchill

    b) Margaret Thatcher

    c) Stephen Hawking

10 Who did Prince William marry in 2012?

    a) Catherine Upperton

    b) Catherine Middleton

    c) Catherine Lowerton

1. What's the nickname for the London Underground?

   a) the Tube   b) the Tunnel   c) the Web

2. Which Ancient Egyptian monument was brought to London in 1870 and stands on the Embankment?

   a) Tutankhamun's Spindle
   b) Cleopatra's Needle
   c) Ramesses's Ramekin

3. The Barbican Estate is a giant housing estate in the heart of London. It was built after the area was devastated by which event?

   a) the Great Plague
   b) the Great Fire
   c) the Blitz

4. The Queen doesn't own a passport.

True or false?

5. Where can you see waxwork replicas of famous people?

   a) Royal Opera House
   b) Madame Tussauds
   c) Tower of London

6. Which city is nearer to London:

Paris or Edinburgh?

7 Which animal can you NOT see at London Zoo?

    a) lion   b) dodo   c) hippo

8 *HMS Belfast* served during the Second World War. It's now a museum ship moored on the River Thames. What are the forward gun turrets aimed at?

    a) a motorway service station

    b) Birmingham

    c) the North Sea

9 Who buried his Parmesan cheese in the back garden during the Great Fire of London, and wrote about it in his diary?

    a) Oliver Cromwell

    b) Isaac Newton

    c) Samuel Pepys

10 The oldest and largest toy store in the world is on Regent Street. What is it called?

    a) Hamleys   b) Toys R Us   c) Harrods

11 Which type of court is used at the Wimbledon tennis championships?

    a) clay   b) hard   c) grass

1 William Shakespeare's *Romeo and Juliet* was first performed in London in the...

a) 1590s   b) 1790s   c) 1990s

2 ... And where was it performed?

a) The Sphere   b) The Globe   c) The Oval

3 In 1939, London's population reached a record 8.61 million. When was that record broken?

a) 1955   b) 1985   c) 2015

4 What's the busiest station on the London Underground?

a) Camden Town   b) Waterloo   c) Whitechapel

5 Princess Diana's funeral took place at Westminster Abbey on September 6th, 1997. How is she sometimes known?

a) the People's Princess
b) the Perfect Princess
c) the Pale Princess

6 The bearskin hats worn by the guards of Buckingham Palace are made from real bear fur.
True or false?

7 If you laid all the lines on the London Underground end to end, they could stretch from London to...

a) Birmingham   b) Manchester   c) Paris

8 Which London landmark was Adolf Hitler going to move to Berlin if Germany conquered Britain?

a) Marble Arch
b) Nelson's Column
c) Buckingham Palace

9 Where can you see thousands of creepy crawlies and a life-size moving model of a *Tyrannosaurus rex*?

a) The Natural History Museum
b) Regent's Park
c) Tate Modern

1. Where can you take a trip through London's history, from prehistoric times to the present day?

a) Science Museum

b) Museum of London

c) London Transport Museum

2. After he was hanged in 1701, which pirate's body was strung up for three years by the River Thames, as a warning to other pirates?

a) Blackbeard   b) Francis Drake   c) Captain Kidd

3. What percentage of the UK's population lives in London?

a) 2.5%   b) 12.5%   c) 25%

4. The City of Westminster is in London.

True or false?

5. In a traditional London café, what's NOT served as part of a full English breakfast?

a) bacon   b) baked beans   c) mushy peas

ALBERT'S CAFE

6 At what age did London chimney sweeps start work in the early 1800s?

    a) 6   b) 10   c) 14

7 What's the busiest shopping street in Europe?

    a) Oxford Street
    b) Downing Street
    c) Fleet Street

8 Where can you see all these inventions?

    a) The British Museum
    b) The Science Museum
    c) The Natural History Museum

9 Which is the most expensive area to live in London?

    a) Brixton
    b) Hackney
    c) Knightsbridge

10 According to the stories, which London barber killed his customers by tipping them from their chair so they fell through a secret trap door?

    a) Jack the Ripper   b) Sweeney Todd   c) Bill Sikes

11 ... And what was his nickname?

    a) the demon barber of Fleet Street
    b) the barbarous barber of Regent Street
    c) the cut-throat clipper of Earl's Court

1. **What's said to haunt the roads around Cambridge Gardens in West London?**

   a) penny farthing   b) taxi   c) double-decker bus

2. **What was unusual about the warrior chieftain called Boudica, who led an uprising against the Romans in 60 AD and burned London to the ground?**

   a) he was 8ft (2.4m) tall
   b) he was blind
   c) she was a woman

3. **London houses are traditionally made from bricks that are...**

   a) yellow   b) white   c) red

4. **What's the name of the concert hall in London that's named after Queen Victoria's husband?**

   a) Royal Alfred Hall
   b) Royal Albert Hall
   c) Royal Archibald Hall

Cockney rhyming slang is a type of London slang where a word is replaced with a phrase that rhymes with it. For example, "dog and bone" means "phone". Sometimes, the end of the phrase is cut off. For example, "loaf of bread" means "head", but you'd say "I banged my loaf".

Can you match each phrase in bold with the correct meaning?

3) "It's all gone **Pete Tong.**"

1) "It's up the **apples and pears.**"

2) "Can you **Adam and Eve** it?"

4) "I'm on my **Jack Jones.**"

5) "You're having a **bubble** mate."

6) "He's telling **porkies.**"

a) believe

b) laugh

7) "Open your **minces.**"

c) eyes

d) own

f) lies

e) stairs

g) wrong

Can you match each name to the right place on the map?

5) The Shard

1) The Globe

3) St Paul's Cathedral

6) Nelson's Column

2) St James's Palace

4) BFI IMAX Cinema

THE WEST END

RIVER THAMES

a

c

b

d

f

Big Ben

St James's Park

e

London Aquarium

Palace of Westminster

Answers

1   **1.** a **2.** false (Istanbul and Moscow both cover a larger area than London.) **3.** b (It's officially called the Elizabeth Tower, and the bell inside is called the Great Bell. But Big Ben is the nickname for both the tower and the bell.) **4.** b (The nickname started because the entrance to the original headquarters was on a street called Great Scotland Yard. The headquarters have since moved to a different location, but the nickname has stuck.) **5.** c **6.** Sherlock Holmes **7.** c **8.** c **9.** b (The average temperature in July is 19.6°C (67.3°F).) **10.** a **11.** a

2   **1.** b **2.** b **3.** a **4.** a (London's first underground line opened in 1863. Beijing in China has the busiest underground system, and Shanghai in China has the longest.) **5.** c **6.** c **7.** b **8.** false (It was bombed nine times.) **9.** b (In the Dungeon, he's played by an actor. The real Jack Sheppard was finally caught and hanged on November 16th, 1724, as crowds of up to 200,000 people lined the streets. He was popular because he'd been born into poverty, like a lot of people at the time, but made fools of the authorities that were oppressing the poor.) **10.** a

3   **1.** the BFG (from the book by Roald Dahl) **2.** b **3.** a **4.** true (The City of London is a small area in the middle of London, measuring just 1.12 square miles (2.9km^2). It's often just called 'The City' to distinguish it from the rest of London. Originally a Celtic settlement, and later occupied by the Romans, it's the oldest part of present-day London. London has grown over the centuries, but The City has kept itself separate, a little city nestled in the heart of London.) **5.** a2, b1 **6.** c (It's given as a token of thanks for Britain's support during the Second World War.) **7.** b **8.** c **9.** c **10.** a

4   **1.** b **2.** c **3.** a **4.** b **5.** b **6.** c **7.** c **8.** a (February only gets 40.9mm (1.6in) of rain. October is the wettest month, with 68.5mm (2.7in).) **9.** a

5   **1.** a **2.** b **3.** b (Its first performance was on October 8th, 1985.) **4.** c (It had 6.7 million visitors in 2013.) **5.** c **6.** b **7.** a **8.** c (It was called 'The Great Manure Crisis of 1894'. There were over 50,000 horses pulling the carriages that transported people around London, and the road sweepers couldn't keep up. But by the early 1900s, cars, trams and buses were increasingly replacing horses, and the problem went away.) **9.** a **10.** b

6   **1.** c **2.** b **3.** c **4.** a **5.** c **6.** b **7.** Peter Pan **8.** Knightsbridge (It's the only station that doesn't have an overground line.) **9.** a **10.** a

7 1. a 2. false (London has 8.7 million people, while Istanbul has 14 million and Moscow has 12.2 million.) 3. c 4. Mary Poppins 5. b (When the Romans united most of Britain in the conquest of 43 AD, they made their capital in 'Camulodunum', which is now called Colchester.) 6. a3, b2, c1 7. b 8. c (Gondolas are used in Venice, Italy.) 9. c 10. true 11. a

8 1. a 2. a 3. c 4. b 5. b 6. a3, b1, c2 7. b 8. false (It's owned by the nation, and so is Windsor Castle. The Queen owns two palaces – Balmoral Castle and Sandringham House.) 9. a 10. c (The disease was spread by fleas that live on rodents, although people at the time didn't know this.)

9 1. c 2. b 3. b 4. b (The Houses make laws and debate important issues.) 5. a 6. c (Emus don't live wild in the UK, and they also can't fly.) 7. a 8. a 9. Victoria Beckham

10 1. a 2. b 3. b 4. c (It's because the sound waves travel around the curved wall.) 5. a 6. a (London's sewage used to flow straight into the River Thames, where it became trapped by tidal currents. The water was thick and foul-smelling, and during a spell of particularly hot weather the stench became so bad that politicians discussed moving Parliament away from London.) 7. b 8. a (Polish is the second most common foreign nationality, with 2% of London's population. Italian is 9th with 0.9%. All the figures are taken from 2014 data.) 9. c 10. c (The heads were dipped in tar and boiled to stop them from rotting. The heads of William Wallace, Thomas More and Oliver Cromwell were all displayed on London Bridge.)

11 1. b 2. a 3. b (Crystal Palace is an area of south London that's named after a huge glass building which stood there from 1854 to 1936, when it burned down.) 4. c 5. c (The main job of the Lord Mayor of the City of London is to campaign for the UK's banking industry.) 6. a4, b2, c1, d3 7. c 8. Oliver Twist (from the story by Charles Dickens) 9. a 10. b (Corpses were left hanging until three tides had washed over their heads.) 11. a 12. left

12 1. a 2. c (The nickname was given to her by a Russian army captain.) 3. true 4. b 5. false (Prime Ministers don't have keys because the door can't be opened from the outside. There's always someone on the inside to unlock it.) 6. a 7. b (Apparently, she said it during dinner after the officer had told a scandalous story. There's no evidence that she did, but the phrase stuck because Victoria was always very stern and serious in public.) 8. c (Raccoons don't live wild in the UK.) 9. b 10. c (The smog was air pollution caused mainly by coal fires and windless weather. It lasted five days and was so thick people could hardly see past the length of their arm. Most of the deaths were due to slow suffocation or lung infections, with many people dying months after the event.) 11. a

13 **1.** red circle with blue bar **2.** c **3.** false (It's a common myth.) **4.** a
5. a **6.** c **7.** b (It was completed in 1984 and cost over £500 million.)
8. a (They don't just wear fancy hats – they wear a whole suit covered
with pearly buttons to raise money for charity. The original Pearly
King was Henry Croft (1861-1930). He was a road sweeper who sewed
mother-of-pearl buttons onto his suit.) **9.** b **10.** b (The Lord Mayor is
the mayor of the City of London – a tiny city in the heart of Greater
London where many banks have their headquarters. A new Lord Mayor
is appointed each year. They parade to the Royal Courts of Justice, to
swear allegiance to the monarch. The parade dates back to the 1500s,
and reflects the wealth and power of the City of London.) **11.** true

14 **1.** a **2.** c **3.** c **4.** b **5.** b (In 2016, it was the fourth most expensive
place to open a store in the world.) **6.** false (For December, January
and February, the average temperature in London is 6.9°C (44.4°F),
and the average temperature in Paris is 5.4°C (41.7°F).) **7.** false (For
June, July and August the average temperature in London is 19.1°C
(66.4°F), and the average temperature in Paris is 19.8°C (67.6°F).) **8.** c
9. a **10.** a **11.** b (He was part of a group of twelve people who plotted
to assassinate King James I of England for his persecution of Catholics.)

15 **1.** a **2.** b (During the Second World War, she joined the women's branch
of the British Army and trained as a driver and mechanic.) **3.** Winnie-
the-Pooh **4.** c **5.** a (The fire burned for four days and destroyed the
homes of over 70,000 people, but only six deaths were recorded. Many
more probably died, but the deaths of poor and middle class people
were not recorded, and also many bodies may have been reduced to
ashes.) **6.** a3, b4, c2, d1 **7.** a (The sculptures were made in the 1850s
and some of them look very strange compared to modern depictions of
dinosaurs.) **8.** b **9.** c **10.** b

16 **1.** a **2.** false (It's Podgorica in Montenegro. On average it has 166cm
(65.4in) of rain each year, compared to London's 56cm (22in).) **3.** a
4. b (The real Dick Whittington was elected Mayor of London four times
between 1397 and 1419, but was never a servant because he came from
a wealthy family.) **5.** b **6.** Daniel Radcliffe **7.** c **8.** c **9.** a **10.** b **11.** c

17 **1.** a (The British Library has every book published in the UK and Ireland
since 1662, giving it the second largest collection of books in the world.
The largest is in the Library of Congress in America.) **2.** c **3.** a (Victoria
reigned from 1837 to 1901. Her husband was Prince Albert.) **4.** b **5.** a
6. c **7.** c **8.** b **9.** a **10.** b

18 1. b 2. c (The full list of sovereign states ruled by the Queen of the UK are: Antigua and Barbuda, Australia, The Bahamas, Barbados, Belize, Canada, Grenada, Jamaica, New Zealand, Papua New Guinea, St. Kitts and Nevis, Saint Lucia, Saint Vincent and the Grenadines, Solomon Islands, Tuvalu and the UK.) 3. a 4. a 5. c 6. b 7. b 8. a (It's short for 'treacle tart', which is Cockney rhyming slang for 'sweetheart'.) 9. c 10. b (Pelicans were introduced to the park in 1664, as a gift from the Russian Ambassador. They're fed fish every day between 2.30pm and 3.00pm.)

19 1. a 2. c (The City of London police is separate to the Metropolitan police that covers the rest of Greater London. Also, the Mayor of Greater London has no authority in the City of London – the City has its own mayor, called The Lord Mayor.) 3. b 4. b 5. a 6. true (Her actual birthday is on April 21st. Her official birthday is usually on the second Saturday in June. It's on a Saturday so that more people can attend the birthday parade, and it's in June so there's a greater chance of good weather.) 7. b (These days it's illegal to have a coal fire in London, because it causes too much air pollution.) 8. c 9. c 10. a 11. b 12. c (It used to be a plaster-cast *Diplodocus* skeleton, but this was replaced by a blue whale skeleton in 2017.)

20 1. c (In 2012, over 20,000 phones were lost – more than 50 a day.) 2. b 3. a 4. c 5. Charlie Chaplin 6. c 7. b 8. true (She's the only person in the UK who can drive without a licence. She learned to drive when she joined the British Army during the Second World War, but she only drives on private roads on her estates. On public roads she has a driver.) 9. a 10. a

21 1. a 2. b 3. a (After committing a robbery in London, he rode to York to 'prove' he couldn't have been in London the night before.) 4. c (The old London Bridge was crammed with tall buildings, including houses, stores and public toilets.) 5. c 6. b 7. c 8. a 9. b

22 1. b 2. false (It's in the southeast.) 3. a 4. b 5. c 6. a 7. b 8. b 9. Banksy 10. c 11. c 12. a (It was a gift from the King of Norway.)

23 1. a (The Normans came from what is now northern France.) 2. false (Three buildings in Moscow are taller.) 3. c 4. a 5. true (Most things cost more in London than in the rest of the country. This is partly because there are lots of rich people in London who can afford to spend more. It's also because lots of companies want to open stores in the city, so landlords can charge more in rent and stores put up their prices to cover the cost.) 6. b 7. a (In 2015, Heathrow served 75 million people, making it the sixth busiest airport in the world.) 8. c 9. a2, b3, c1 10. b 11. a 12. c (Strawberries and cream are traditionally eaten by spectators at Wimbledon.)

24 **1.** false (It's an area of London that used to have a big fruit-and-veg market, and is home to the Royal Opera House.) **2.** c (London's sewage used to flow into the River Thames at a point where people also got their drinking water. This filthy water carried a disease called 'cholera', which had already killed over 30,000 people between 1831 and 1854. So Bazalgette designed a huge network of underground sewers, over 1,300 miles (2,092km) long, that carried the sewage away from London and deposited it into the Thames further downstream. Since the network was completed, there has never been another outbreak of cholera in London. Later, Bazalgette designed sewage treatment works to purify the sewage before the liquid flowed back into the Thames.) **3.** the *Cutty Sark* **4.** a **5.** b **6.** a **7.** c (Some say the King feared an uprising from Blood's followers, while others think he had a fondness for scoundrels.) **8.** c **9.** b (She went on to become Britain's first female Prime Minister.) **10.** b

25 **1.** a **2.** b **3.** c **4.** true (In a British passport, it asks that the owner be allowed to pass in the name of the Queen. The Queen doesn't need to ask in the name of herself, so she doesn't need a passport.) **5.** b **6.** Paris (Edinburgh is over 100 miles (160km) farther away.) **7.** b (It's extinct!) **8.** a (The guns aren't loaded, and the target was only chosen to show how far the guns could fire. They have a range of 14 miles (23km), which isn't far enough to hit the other two targets.) **9.** c (At the time, Parmesan cheese was very expensive because it was so rare in England.) **10.** a (It opened in 1760.) **11.** c

26 **1.** a **2.** b **3.** c (In 2015, the population reached 8.63 million, the first time the population was higher than in 1939.) **4.** b **5.** a **6.** true **7.** c **8.** b **9.** a

27 **1.** b **2.** c **3.** b (Over 1 in 10 people living in the UK live in London.) **4.** true (The City of Westminster was founded in the 1000s. Originally it was separate from London, but as they expanded they merged into one. But Westminster is still its own city, nestled in the heart of London.) **5.** c **6.** a (Young children could shimmy up the narrow chimneys.) **7.** a **8.** b **9.** c (In 2015, the average house price in Knightsbridge was £3.5 million.) **10.** b **11.** a

28 **1.** c **2.** c **3.** a **4.** b

29 **1.** e **2.** a **3.** g **4.** d **5.** b (short for 'bubble bath') **6.** f (short for 'pork pies') **7.** c (short for 'mince pies')

30 **1.** j **2.** d **3.** g **4.** f **5.** k **6.** b **7.** i **8.** h **9.** l **10.** a **11.** e **12.** c

First published in 2017 by Usborne Publishing Ltd, 83–85 Saffron Hill, London ECIN 8RT, England.